# GREAT MINDS OF SCIENCE

# Rachel Carson

## Ecologist and Activist

Mary Gow

**Enslow Publishers, Inc.**

40 Industrial Road                    PO Box 38
Box 398                                   Aldershot
Berkeley Heights, NJ 07922   Hants GU12 6BP
USA                                              UK

http://www.enslow.com

*To Lizzy*

**Library of Congress Cataloging-in-Publication Data**

Gow, Mary.
 Rachel Carson : ecologist and activist / by Mary Gow.— 1st ed.
 p. cm.
 Includes bibliographical references and index.
 ISBN 0-7660-2503-9
 1. Carson, Rachel, 1907–1964—Juvenile literature. 2. Biologists—United
States—Biography—Juvenile literature. 3. Environmentalists—United States—
Biography—Juvenile literature. I. Title.
 QH31.C33A42 2005
 570'.92—dc22
                                                    2004030794

Printed in the United States of America

032011 The HF Group, North Manchester, IN

10 9 8 7 6 5 4 3 2

**To Our Readers:**
We have done our best to make sure all Internet Addresses in this book were active and
appropriate when we went to press. However, the author and the publisher have no
control over and assume no liability for the material available on those Internet sites
or on other Web sites they may link to. Any comments or suggestions can be sent by
e-mail to comments@enslow.com or to the address on the back cover.

**Illustration Credits:** Carson family photograph, used by permission of the
Rachel Carson Council, Inc., p. 17; Courtesy of Chatham College, Pittsburgh,
Pennsylvania/ Rachel Carson Institute, p. 29; Photo by New Bedford
Standard Times, used by permission of the Rachel Carson Council, Inc., p. 8;
Photograph by Mary Frye, used by permission of the Rachel Carson Council,
Inc., p. 33; Photographed by Bob Hines, used with permission of the Rachel
Carson Council, Inc., p. 89; Photographer John Bortniak, courtesy of the
National Oceanic and Atmospheric Administration (NOAA), p. 35; Regina
Greenwood, p. 68; Royce Collection, New England Fisheries (NOAA), p. 55;
State Archives of Florida, p. 72; Steven Hewitt, pp. 77, 103; U.S. Army Signal
Corps, pp. 64, 70; U.S. Fish and Wildlife Service, pp. 12, 43, 48, 52, 58, 83,
94; Used by permission of the Rachel Carson Council, Inc., p. 21.

**Cover Illustration:** U.S. Fish and Wildlife Service

Selections from the published works of Rachel Carson: "Undersea" in the *Atlantic
Monthly* Magazine Copyright © September, 1937 by R. L. Carson, p. 40; *Silent Spring*
by Rachel Carson Copyright © 1962 by Rachel L. Carson, Copyright © renewed 1984
by Roger Christie Reprinted by permission of Frances Collin, Trustee, pp. 75–76.

# Contents

# Deadly Consequences

EVERY YEAR IN THE EARLY SPRING, TINY RED and green flowers blossomed on the stately elm trees at Michigan State University. Every spring even before the elms bloomed, red-breasted robins flew back to the campus after wintering in the south. The sight of robins hopping on the lawns pulling worms from the earth was a sure sign that warmer weather was on the way. Year after year, the robins returned and built their twiggy nests around the campus. Soon, elm leaves would unfurl and baby birds would join their parents on the college green.

In 1955, the robins returned and the early birds again got their worms. Soon, though, it was clear that something was horribly wrong. All around the

Michigan State campus, students and faculty found dead and dying robins. The birds suffered tremors and convulsions before dying.[1] Spring progressed as trees budded and burst into leaf, but few baby birds were seen.

The following year, when spring's warmth eased out the winter chill, robins returned and robins died. The next year, 1957, brought yet another wave of death. In the spring and summer of 1958 not a single young living robin was seen on the Michigan State campus.[2]

At the same time that robins were expiring in Michigan, other birds and animals in North America were meeting a similar untimely fate. Cardinals, quail, sparrows, and rabbits died in Georgia.[3] In Wisconsin, screech owls and little warblers perished. Trout and salmon floated lifelessly in Canada's Miramachi River. Countless crabs and more than one million fish died in the salt marshes along one section of Florida's coast.[4] In nesting areas and on migratory routes, people saw fewer and fewer bald eagles and ospreys. Young eaglets and osprey chicks became increasingly rare.

These wildlife tragedies of the late 1950s occurred in different states and in different seasons, but they were all linked. All resulted from mankind's use of newly developed, long-lasting, deadly poisons called pesticides. The first of these pesticides, dichloro-diphenyl-trichloroethane, was known as DDT. In the 1950s, DDT and other related chemicals were used widely on public and private land in efforts to kill insect pests like mosquitoes and fire ants. The pesticides, however, often had unintended effects.

In 1962, the American public was awakened to these tragedies and the dangers of pesticides by the words of a soft-spoken scientist named Rachel Carson. A skilled biologist and an eloquent author, Rachel Carson wrote a powerful book called *Silent Spring*. In it she showed how Americans were poisoning their environment and endangering nature and themselves with irresponsible use of pesticides. *Silent Spring* became one of the most influential books of the twentieth century.[5]

Carson's sensitivity to nature and her literary fluency were rooted in her childhood. Born in 1907, in rural Pennsylvania, Carson was outdoors observing birds, insects, and other animals as a youngster. An early reader who was fond of animal books, Carson was soon writing her own stories. She was only eleven years old when her first story was

*Rachel Carson holds a starfish over an aquarium at the Woods Hole Oceanographic Institute in 1953.*

published in a national magazine. Carson expected to be a writer, but was drawn to biology in college and became a scientist. She earned her master's degree in zoology, a rare achievement for a young woman in the early 1930s.

Carson had a distinguished professional career as a marine biologist for the U. S. Fish and Wildlife Service. While working full-time for the government, her creativity found an outlet in the nature writing she did at night and on weekends. Overcoming obstacles of limited time and considerable family responsibilities, she built a second career for herself as an acclaimed author. Carson wrote three best-selling books about the sea.

An ecological theme ran through Carson's books. Ecology is the branch of biology that deals with relationships of living things to each other and to their environment. The word ecology is derived from the ancient Greek words *oikos*, meaning house, and *logos*, meaning study. Ecology can be roughly translated as the study of the home. Scientists talked and wrote about ecology from the late 1800s, but the term was not widely used until the 1960s.

Ecology deals with such relationships as food chains. This is a way to explain how energy is transferred from plants to the animals that eat them, then on to other animals, and then back to the environment. One example of a food chain is an elm leaf that falls to the ground and is eaten by an earthworm. The earthworm is then eaten by a robin, and the unlucky robin is consumed by a hungry housecat. In another food chain, green algae grows in a pond. Mosquito larvae on the pond's surface eat the algae. A trout swimming in the pond eats mosquito larvae, and an eagle flies down and devours the trout. In the food-chain process, when the housecat, eagle, or other predator dies and decays, its body's materials provide nutrients for life on the land or in the water and the cycle begins anew.

Through Carson's sensitive writing, she showed how food chains worked and how webs of life were interconnected. Carson's readers learned scientific facts while enjoying the poetry of her words. For many, her books heightened their appreciation of the beauty and value of nature.

When DDT was first sold, Carson was concerned that it could upset the balance of nature.[6] DDT and related chemicals were intended to do good, by killing pests that damaged farm crops or carried disease. But these pesticides had a dark side. They often killed things we want to keep alive. They also lasted a long time in the water and soil, continuing to poison other life even after killing the pests they targeted. Understanding food chains, Carson could see how pesticides could endanger living things that had not even come directly in contact with them. If an eagle ate a fish that had eaten mosquitoes sprayed by pesticide, the eagle was consuming the pesticide. Even if the eagle had been many miles away when the mosquitoes' pond was sprayed, the bird still got a dose of the poison.

In the 1950s, the use of pesticides expanded rapidly. Tons of DDT and related chemicals were sprayed on fields, forests, beaches, and wetlands from airplanes and trucks. Carson heard about wildlife tragedies where birds, fish, and other living things died after spraying. She believed that the pesticides were poisoning the environment. She recognized that people could not poison the land for other living things without being affected themselves.

For four years Carson collected facts and studies about pesticides. She learned their chemistry. She read wildlife studies from places that had been

*In 1955, after the pesticide dichloro-diphenyl-trichloroethane (DDT)
was sprayed on elm trees at Michigan State University, adult robins
died on the campus and few chicks survived to leave their nests.*

sprayed. She consulted experts who knew about insects, human health, soil, and water. Finally, in her clear poetic voice, Carson wove the scientific facts together into her compelling book, *Silent Spring*.

*Silent Spring* sounded a loud alarm about the dangers of pesticides. But Carson's goal was not just to shock people about the horrors of reckless pesticide use. She wanted readers to take action and stop the misuse of pesticides.[7] She wanted people to recognize that we share the planet with other life forms and should act responsibly rather than arrogantly trying to control nature.[8]

# Childhood in Nature

RACHEL CARSON WAS BORN IN THE springtime. The countryside around her family's western Pennsylvania home teemed with new life. Baby gray squirrels ventured out of tree hollows into the sunshine. Red fox kits peeked out from dens. Meadows and woods were filled with birdsong. By the time Rachel entered the world on May 27, 1907, migratory birds, including scarlet tanagers and Baltimore orioles, had flown back to Pennsylvania after wintering in South America. Robins returned earlier in the season. By late May, their first chirping broods were already out of the nest.

From the time she was born, nature and the outdoors shaped Rachel Carson's life. Her home was in a rural area with fields, forests, creeks, and steep bluffs. Fish swam in the streams. Garter snakes slipped through the grass. Living creatures were part of her world, and with her mother's guidance, Rachel was raised to see and value them.

Rachel Carson's family lived on a hillside in the little town of Springdale, Pennsylvania. The Carsons were not farmers, but they kept a few animals— chickens, sheep, and pigs. Apple and pear trees grew in their orchard. Farm buildings, including a small barn, stood near the house. Their little outhouse was nearby; the Carsons' home had no indoor plumbing. During her childhood, Carson's hometown was clean and rural. However, not all of western Pennsylvania was pristine.

Downstream on the Allegheny River, about fifteen miles from Springdale, was Pittsburgh, known as the steel capital of the world. In the late 1800s the steel industry boomed. Huge mills were built along the Allegheny, the Ohio, and the Monongahela, the three rivers that meet in Pittsburgh. The mills burned mountains of coal and used tons of iron ore. Great smokestacks poured clouds of pollution over the city. The steel mills dumped industrial chemicals into the rivers. Pittsburgh and the steel industry were growing when Rachel was born.

Rachel's parents, Robert and Maria McLean Carson, bought their Springdale house and sixty-four acres of land in 1900. The Carsons probably anticipated Pittsburgh's growth when they chose their home. As Pittsburgh grew, more families might want to live in Springdale and land there would become more valuable. Robert Carson later advertised building lots for sale and eventually sold some, but his land development plan was not a success.

Robert Carson was born near Pittsburgh in 1864, during the Civil War. As a young man he sang in a Presbyterian church choir. Photographs show that he was a slender and attractive man with a well-groomed mustache. Through the years Robert Carson held many different jobs. He worked as a clerk, an insurance salesman, an electrician, and also as a supervisor in a power station, but he was not very successful. At times Robert Carson had financial problems that left his family living on the edge of poverty.

Rachel's mother was also from western Pennsylvania. The daughter of a minister, Maria

*Maria Carson with her three children, Marian, Rachel, and Robert.*

McLean was well-educated for a woman at that time. She graduated from the Washington Female Seminary, a private Presbyterian high school. A serious student, she took some college level courses. Musically talented, Maria sang, played piano, and composed music. As a young woman, she taught school and gave piano lessons. In 1893, she met Robert Carson at a choral event where they both were singing. When they married, Maria stopped teaching school.

Rachel was the youngest of Maria and Robert's three children. Their eldest, Marian, was ten years old when Rachel was born; their son, Robert, was eight. With the older children already in school, Maria had time to enjoy her baby daughter.

Maria Carson loved the outdoors. She liked bird-watching and was an amateur naturalist. She shared her fondness for the natural world with her family. From Rachel's early months, Maria spent time with her outside. When Rachel was just a toddler, mother and daughter took walks together in the fields and woods around their home. Maria taught her about plants and animals. As Rachel grew, the two discussed what they saw.[1]

In exploring the outdoors with Rachel, Maria

Carson had some assistance. In the early 1900s, a respected group of educators believed that children should grow up in touch with nature. Liberty Hyde Bailey, a Cornell University professor, was one of the founders of the nature-study movement. "The result of nature-study teaching is the development of a keen personal interest in every natural object and phenomenon," wrote Bailey in 1903.[2] "If one is to be happy, he must be in sympathy with common things. He must live in harmony with his environment," Bailey explained.[3]

Many nature-study books and lessons were published. Anna Botsford Comstock, one of the first female professors at Cornell University, published her *Handbook of Nature Study* in 1911. The book was filled with lessons about birds, fish, insects, mammals, reptiles, and plants. The lessons could be led by parents or teachers. They guided children through observations of the habits of bluebirds, the song of crickets, the agile flight of bats, and much more.

The nature-study movement was ahead of its time, when understanding of the environment was far different than it is today. For many years, the land and nature of North America seemed boundless.

Thoughtlessly, natural resources and native animals were destroyed. Forests were clear-cut to open land for farming and for lumber to build cities and railroads. Water sources, like Pittsburgh's rivers, were polluted by industrial waste. Wildlife suffered as animals were hunted without concern for their numbers. As many as sixty million American bison reportedly grazed the western plains in the 1700s, but so many were killed that fewer than one thousand remained in 1889.[4]

During her lifetime, Maria Carson witnessed one of America's great wildlife tragedies—extinction of a species, the passenger pigeon. Species extinction means that the species ceases to exist—the last of its kind dies. Some species extinctions occur naturally. Dinosaurs became extinct millions of years ago through some accidental occurrence. In recent history, though, increasing numbers of species have become extinct because of irresponsible human actions.

Growing up, Maria Carson would have seen great flocks of passenger pigeons that flew between Canada and the Gulf of Mexico each year. Millions of these gray-blue birds migrated through Pennsylvania, darkening the sky as they passed

*Rachel Carson as a child, reading to her dog, Candy.*

overhead. In flight, the flocks were often more than a mile wide and many miles long. The pigeons nested together, sometimes building more than one hundred nests in a single tree. Passenger pigeons were tasty to eat and easy to hunt. People slaughtered them by the millions. The pigeons' numbers also declined as forests were cut down and the birds had fewer places to live and find food. The last flocks of passenger pigeons in Pennsylvania were seen in the late 1880s. The last passenger pigeon in the world died in a zoo in Cincinnati in 1914.[5] Knowing the passenger pigeon's plight may have heightened Maria Carson's reverence for nature.

Besides teaching Rachel about the natural world, Maria Carson introduced her to the world of books. Rachel learned to read when she was very young. She enjoyed books about animals, including Beatrix Potter's *Peter Rabbit* and Kenneth Grahame's *Wind in the Willows*.[6] Growing up, she read Gene Stratton Porter's novels. Porter, author of *Laddie* and *A Girl of the Limberlost*, expressed views similar to those of the nature-study movement.

At a young age, Rachel Carson started writing her own stories. As a preschooler, she made a little book for her father with poems and pictures of animals. Maria Carson helped her daughter with the project, but Rachel wrote out many of the words and colored in the pictures.[7] When she was about eight years old, she wrote "The Little Brown House," a story about two wrens seeking a home and finding the perfect birdhouse. She was a bit older when she wrote "A Sleeping Rabbit" and illustrated it with a sweet picture of a dozing bunny.

Besides the many books she read, one magazine especially influenced Rachel, *St. Nicholas for Boys and Girls*. Every month, *St. Nicholas* published a superb combination of stories and nonfiction articles. Biographies of artists, reports on inventions, and news of scientific discoveries were all regularly in the magazine. Some of the finest stories for children written at the time appeared in *St. Nicholas*. Mark Twain, Louisa May Alcott, Rudyard Kipling, and Joseph Conrad were among the magazine's contributors.

A regular feature of the magazine was the "St. Nicholas League." Young readers sent their poems, stories, drawings, photographs, and puzzles to the magazine. Several of their submissions were published each month. A gold badge and a silver badge were awarded in each category. Rachel Carson was eleven years old when she first had a story published in the "St. Nicholas League."

Rachel's brother, Robert, gave her the inspiration for her story. Robert had enlisted in the U. S. Army Air Service in 1917. World War I was raging and he went to serve in France. In his letters, he told his family about his experiences in the war. In one letter, he wrote about a heroic Canadian flight instructor.[8]

Moved by his tale, Rachel wrote "A Battle in the Clouds." She mailed it to *St. Nicholas*. In September 1918, her story was in the magazine and honored with a silver badge.

Inspired by her success, Rachel wrote and sent more stories to *St. Nicholas*. "A Young Hero (or Heroine)," "A Message to the Front," and "A Famous Sea Fight" were all published within the next year. Winning gold and silver badges, Rachel became an "Honor Member" of the "St. Nicholas League" and earned a $10 cash award when she was twelve years old.

As an adult, Rachel commented that she had been a solitary child. Her family's home was some distance from the town center, so few potential friends were nearby. The Carsons' money worries may also have isolated her. While she may not have had children to play with, she grew up in the company of books, the outdoors, pet dogs, and her supportive mother.

Maria Carson could see her daughter's keen intellect and writing talent. She wanted Rachel to have the benefits of education, but Springdale had no high school. Rachel's brother and sister ended their formal education after tenth grade. To finish high school, Rachel commuted by trolley to the town of Parnassus, several miles away. She graduated from Parnassus High School in 1925 with the highest grades in her class.

# 3

# Becoming a Scientist

EIGHTEEN-YEAR-OLD RACHEL CARSON arrived at the Pennsylvania College for Women with dreams and determination. She planned to major in English and become a writer.[1] Located in Pittsburgh, the college was housed in a grand mansion on the sweeping grounds of a former private estate. The school had a good academic reputation.

Paying for Rachel's college education was a challenge for her family. She won a scholarship competition that paid part of her tuition and the Carsons supplemented that by selling some land. Rachel's mother, Maria, so valued her daughter's education that she sold silver and china from her parents and she took on more piano students.[2] The president of the college also arranged an additional private scholarship for Rachel because she believed that Rachel was a very promising student.[3]

Beginning in her first year, Rachel studied English composition with Miss Grace Croff, a bright and challenging professor. Rachel wrote many fine pieces as assignments for Croff's classes. Several of them were published in the school's literary journal. During her freshman year she wrote "The Master of the Ship's Light," a story set on the seacoast. Rachel had never seen the ocean, but her writing created clear images of the sea. Professor Croff praised her style and commended her for making technical information in the story interesting.[4] Many years later Rachel's writing would be acclaimed for that same quality.

In college, Rachel was not unfriendly, but she kept to herself. She was quiet and not inclined to participate in social events like tea parties and dances. She worked on the school newspaper and played field hockey and basketball. Although Rachel lived at the college, she kept her close ties to her mother. On weekends Maria Carson often visited her daughter, bringing treats like homemade cookies.

The Pennsylvania College for Women required

all students to take at least one year of science. In her sophomore year Rachel enrolled in biology, taught by Miss Mary Scott Skinker. Biology is the science of living things. For Rachel, who was already passionate about nature, biology offered a way to understand some of life's mysteries. In Professor Skinker's class, Rachel learned how living cells did different jobs. In the biology laboratory she could see tiny organisms through a microscope—life forms that she could not see with her unassisted eye. Skinkers' classes were not always confined to the lecture hall and laboratory. She sometimes took students on field trips into the countryside.

A dynamic and energetic teacher, Mary Scott Skinker became a role model and mentor to Rachel, who thrived in her class. She discovered a science that captured her imagination. She found a teacher who inspired her and who would later help her build a career in science. In biology class, she also found friends who shared her interests. Taking Skinker's biology class was a turning point in Rachel's life. Inspired by the subject and teacher, she decided to change her major course of study from English to biology.

Rachel did not make the decision to change her

*Rachel Carson's yearbook photo from the Pennsylvania College for Women, taken in 1928.*

major easily. Her dream had been to be a writer. She went to college with that goal. Biology, though, beckoned more strongly. From a practical point of view, Rachel faced a dilemma. At the time, writing and teaching English were accepted careers for women, while few women worked as scientists.

When Rachel looked back on her struggle to decide between science and writing, she observed, "I thought I had to be one or the other; it never occurred to me, or apparently to anyone else, that I could combine the two careers."[5] Many years passed before she discovered how brilliantly she could merge her two passions.

Besides discovering biology, another experience at college made a powerful impression on Rachel. One night a violent thunderstorm passed over Pittsburgh. Rachel was in her dormitory room in the mansion reading a poem called "Locksley Hall" by Alfred Lord Tennyson. A line from the poem reads, "For the mighty wind arises, roaring seaward, and I go." Years later, Rachel recalled that those words on that night seemed to tell her that her future was bound to the sea.[6]

Although she lived far from the coast, Rachel had been intrigued by the ocean from childhood. She read sea-themed books by Joseph Conrad and Herman Melville. She once told college friends about finding fossils of fish in rocks near her home and that they had captured her imagination. Along with science and literature, the sea would play a defining role in Rachel Carson's life.

In June 1929, Rachel graduated from the Pennsylvania College for Women with high academic honors. A friend wrote in her yearbook, "Rachel, I want you to remember what I told you about a wild lady biologist. Remember that I prophesy you'll be a famous author yet. Please don't take all the frogs and skeletons too seriously."[7]

After graduation, with guidance from Mary Scott Skinker, Rachel had an exciting future planned. She returned to Springdale briefly and then headed east to the sea to continue her education. She would spend the summer at the Marine Biological Laboratory in Massachusetts, just as Skinker had. In the fall she would begin studying for her master's degree in biology at Johns Hopkins University in Baltimore, Maryland.

The Marine Biological Laboratory is an independent educational center located on the ocean in Woods Hole on Cape Cod. Since 1888, it has provided a place for biologists to do research. Rachel and her friend Mary Frye, a fellow biology student, were both attending its summer program. Carson was there as a beginning investigator, continuing a study of reptile nerves that she had started in college. Rachel and Mary lived together in a nearby boarding house. The Marine Biological Laboratory was known for its friendly and intellectual atmosphere. Students and scientists there shared their enthusiasm for their subjects. They worked on their own projects, but ate their meals together. Sometimes they socialized at parties or picnics on the beach.

In Woods Hole, Rachel's fascination with the sea flourished. She spent hours outdoors on the shore. Rachel peered into the pools of sea water left when the tide went out, searching for creatures who made tidepools their homes. One day she went out on the *Albatross II*, a research ship, collecting marine specimens with other scientists. Some nights she went to the shore to watch the ocean by moonlight. Rachel would return to Woods Hole many times throughout her life.

After her seaside summer, Rachel began graduate school at Johns Hopkins University. She

*Rachel Carson at Woods Hole in 1929 on a Fish and Wildlife Service marine research vessel.*

was studying zoology, the branch of biology that deals with animals. She had won a scholarship to pay for her tuition.

Rachel had barely started at Johns Hopkins when a national economic disaster rocked the nation. In late October 1929, the prices of stocks in American companies plummeted. The Stock Market Crash of 1929 was a dramatic symptom of the Great Depression that was rapidly engulfing the nation.

Within weeks of the crash, many businesses failed and unemployment around the country soared.

During this uncertain time, Rachel saw that Baltimore seemed to have more jobs than western Pennsylvania.[8] She also probably missed her mother—it was the longest time the two had ever been apart. That winter, Rachel rented a house near Baltimore and prepared for her family to come live with her. Her parents arrived in the spring of 1930. Rachel's sister Marian and her two young daughters followed in June. The house was crowded, but at least all the Carsons could share expenses.

Rachel was happy at Johns Hopkins taking challenging courses and doing research. But in her second year there, she had to change her plans. Tuition at the university had increased but her scholarship had not. To make ends meet, she decided to study part-time and work part-time. For her job, she did research on fruit flies and rats in the laboratory of a famous scientist, Raymond Pearl.

In early 1931, Rachel's brother sold the family house in Springdale and came to Baltimore. After he found work repairing radios, Robert brought some unexpected joy into Rachel's life. One day, one of Robert's customers paid him with a Persian cat and

*Rachel Carson first studied at the Marine Biological Laboratory in Woods Hole, Massachusetts, in 1929. She returned there many times as she wrote her eloquent books about the sea. This picturesque seaside town is still a vibrant center for marine research.*

kittens. Rachel had been fond of dogs as a child. When Robert gave her Buzzie, Kito, and Timmy Tiptoes, Rachel began many years as a devoted cat owner.[9]

Rachel Carson was awarded her master's degree in zoology from Johns Hopkins University in 1932. She expected to continue her studies. Again, the economic hardships of the times interfered. In 1934, Carson withdrew from Johns Hopkins to try to find a full-time job.

# Writing, Science, and Government Work

HER COLLEGE BIOLOGY PROFESSOR, MARY
Scott Skinker, played an important role in Rachel
Carson's decision to become a biologist. Skinker had
helped Carson with suggestions about studying at
Woods Hole and Johns Hopkins University. As
Carson started her career during the challenging
times of the Great Depression, Skinker again offered
some valuable advice. By then, Skinker had left
college teaching and was working in the Zoological
Division of the U. S. Department of Agriculture in
Washington, D.C. As Washington was barely forty
miles from Baltimore, the two friends saw each other
often. Skinker suggested that Carson consider
working for the government, too.[1]

In 1935, Carson took the civil service examination required to get a job as a government wildlife biologist. Skinker then urged her to visit Elmer Higgins to apply for a position. Higgins was chief of the Division of Scientific Inquiry in the U. S. Bureau of Fisheries. The Bureau of Fisheries did surveys and recommended management of food fish in the country's coastal waters, lakes, rivers, and streams.

Higgins had no open jobs for biologists. However, he had a project in his office that was not going well. The Bureau of Fisheries was producing short radio programs to teach the public about marine life. The programs were titled "Romance Under the Waters," but scientists in Higgins' office called them "Seven-Minute Fish Tales."[2] Although he did not know Carson's writing ability, Higgins hired her to prepare some scripts. When he read them, he was so pleased that he hired her to write the rest of the series.[3]

Some of Carson's scripts were about local species, like shad, a popular food fish. Shad fishing was a big business in the Chesapeake Bay. Baltimore, where Carson was living, is located near the Chesapeake. As Carson learned about shad for her radio script, she saw that some of the information would make an interesting feature story for a newspaper.[4] She wrote an article, "It'll Be Shad Time Soon," and sent it to the *Baltimore Sun* newspaper. In the story she explained how shad are born in the fresh water of rivers but migrate to the ocean where they live in salt water for most of their lives. To reproduce, adult shad travel hundreds of miles using an amazing homing instinct to return to the river where they were born. The *Baltimore Sun* bought her article and published it in March 1936. She would soon also write about ducks, oysters, eels, starlings, and other local wildlife for the newspaper.

After the radio scripts, Higgins asked Carson to write a general piece about the sea. When Higgins read Carson's essay, he suggested that she send it to the *Atlantic Monthly*.[5] The *Atlantic Monthly* was, and is, a magazine known for its intelligent and engaging articles.

When a position for a wildlife biologist in the Bureau of Fisheries opened in 1936, Carson was hired. At last she had a full-time job. In the Bureau, she was one of only two female biologists. Research and field positions at that time were generally reserved for men. In her job, Carson analyzed fish studies and wrote reports and brochures about fish conservation.

Conservation is the care, protection, and management of natural resources. Fish conservation requires understanding what fish need to survive. Fish populations can be endangered if too many fish are caught or if they do not have enough food. Environmental factors like pollution or change in water temperature affect fish.

Carson's government duties required her to travel around Chesapeake Bay. She consulted with conservation experts and met with fishermen. When she traveled, Carson kept detailed notes about fish, birds, weather, and the landscape that she saw.[6]

From the time Carson was hired by the Bureau of Fisheries, she led a double life. For most of the next fifteen years, she spent her days working as a government scientist and her nights and weekends writing about nature. Along with her articles for the *Baltimore Sun*, soon she was also writing a book.

Besides her work commitments, Carson had considerable responsibilities at home. Sadness had struck her family twice. Her father died in the summer of 1935. Two years later her sister Marian died of pneumonia. Marian had two daughters;

eleven-year-old Marjorie and twelve-year-old Virginia. Carson and her mother would raise Marian's girls. The family of two women and two girls moved into a house in Silver Spring, Maryland. Their new home was convenient to schools and was just a short drive to Carson's downtown Washington, D.C., office. Carson's mother, Maria, cooked, cleaned, and managed the house. Rachel Carson was the family's sole breadwinner.

During this time of financial worry and family adjustments, Carson revised her essay and sent it to the *Atlantic Monthly*, as Higgins had suggested.[7] "Undersea," was published in September 1937. Besides earning Carson $100, a welcome addition to her income, the article also launched her literary career.

"Who has known the ocean? Neither you nor I, with our earthbound senses, know the foam and surge of the tide that beats over the crab hiding under the seaweed of his tide-pool home," her article opened.[8]

In "Undersea" Carson presented the ocean from the perspective of sea creatures rather than humans. She described the cold, dark, and crushing pressure of the depths of the sea. She wrote about starfish, crabs, and anemones that live in tide pools, pounded twice daily by rising tides. Carson told about sharks and whales and also microscopic diatoms, tiny algae that are the food source for most sea life. The article gave readers a feeling of the sea and a sense of its natural cycles.

Carson's beautifully written story impressed two influential *Atlantic* readers. Hendrik Villem van Loon, an internationally famous writer and illustrator, sent Carson a letter expressing his admiration for her article. Quincy Howe, an editor at a publishing company, also wrote to Carson. Howe wondered whether she planned to write a book about the sea. Moved by their encouraging words, Carson almost immediately started writing her first book.

Carson's double life became busier. Her book required a great deal of research. In her government job she was promoted and had new responsibilities. During this time, the Bureau of Fisheries became part of a new, larger government agency, the Fish and Wildlife Service.

For her book, Carson drew on her scientific knowledge and on her personal observations of the sea. Research that she had done earlier, including her work on shad and a study of eels that she did in college, took new shape as she wrote. She also sought out new experiences. During each of the three summers while she was writing *Under the Sea Wind*, Carson went to the ocean. The first year she took her mother and nieces to Beaufort, North Carolina. Carson explored the beaches there by day and night. She visited marsh pools and ponds. On her walks she listened to the calls of the shorebirds and the sound of the surf. She felt the sand under her feet and the sea breeze brushing her skin. She kept notes about the smells and sights of the shore.[9] The Carolina coast would become the setting for a portion of her book. Carson went back to Woods Hole for each of the other two summers. In the research library there, she could track down elusive details about her marine subjects. At Woods Hole, she could also observe the coast and its life.

Writing *Under the Sea Wind* took Carson more than three years. With her government job and family responsibilities, often her only quiet times were late at night. Two of her cats, Buzzie and Kito, frequently kept her company, sitting on her papers as she wrote.

In *Under the Sea Wind*, the creatures that lived in

*Rachel Carson's government photograph taken while she was working for the United States Fish and Wildlife Service in 1944.*

or near the sea were the characters. Except for a few fishermen, humans were barely featured in it. She organized the book in three parts, "The Edge of the Sea," "The Gulls's Way," and "River and Sea." In each section she followed migrating animals and showed the environments they passed through.

Carson wrote about the animals personally, but without anthropomorphizing, or humanizing, them. She focused on individuals. She offered glimpses of the life of a single mackerel in the school of thousands of shimmering silver fish. She showed the toll of a late Arctic snowstorm on a pair of snowy owls. For certain animals, she adapted their scientific names to be personal names. The scientific name for the black skimmer is *Rynchops nigris*. Black skimmers are coastal birds with long pointed beaks that fly low over the water, skimming fish from just below the surface for their food. Following the bird she named Rynchops, Carson showed the skimmers' nesting ground on the Carolina coast.

In a gentle poetic way, Carson told about migrations and cycles of life. She told how shad swim from the sea to breed in freshwater rivers. She followed Anguilla, the eel, in his opposite migration. Certain eels breed in the deep salt water of the

Atlantic, but live the rest of the time in the ponds and marshes of the shore. Carson told how in their daily lives creatures hunt and are hunted. She eloquently showed food chains at work. She wrote about terrapins, for example, nibbling on marsh grass. Nearby, a baby terrapin who had just hatched, was eaten by a rat. A large heron then devoured the rat.[10] She presented life and death as part of the reality of nature in harmony.

Carson's *Under the Sea Wind* was published in November 1941. Reviewers praised its poetic style and accurate science. But before many readers had bought it, international events took their attention elsewhere. On December 7, Japanese airplanes bombed U. S. Navy ships in Pearl Harbor, Hawaii. The United States entered World War II. *Under the Sea Wind* was set aside in the global turmoil.

# Writing the Sea

DURING WORLD WAR II, RACHEL CARSON'S successful government career advanced. She was promoted and was responsible for more Fish and Wildlife Service publications. Some of these were for scientists and others for the public.

One of Carson's projects was a series of booklets called "Food from the Sea." In wartime, much of the country's beef and other meat was sent to feed soldiers, making it scarcer at home. American families began eating more seafood. Cod, haddock, and a few other fish were popular dinner foods. Because of their popularity, these species were in danger of being overfished. The booklets encouraged families to try other, less familiar seafood.

Carson carried out her assignment for "Food from the Sea" with her own special flair. In "The Clam," Carson wrote about clam embryos, only one-three-hundredth of an inch long, spinning through coastal waters. She described dangers that the tiny clams faced from jellyfish, crabs, and starfish. She explained how mature clams burrowed into the sand, spending most of their adult lives buried there.[1] Housewives who read her informative bulletins found recipes and nutritional information, but they also learned about life in the ocean.

In her limited free time, Carson continued writing, but did not start a new book. After three years of work, *Under the Sea Wind* had earned her praise but little money. Carson instead began writing nature articles for magazines. Her story, "The Bat Knew It First," explained the navigation sonar system of this nocturnal flying mammal. Telling how bats use echoes to sense the location of insects, she taught the principles of radar. Radar was a new wartime technology widely used to detect locations of ships and aircraft. Carson's story was published in *Reader's Digest* and was even used by the U. S. Navy to explain radar to sailors.

Carson's day job carried increasing responsibilities

CONSERVATION
IN ACTION

GUARDING OUR
WILDLIFE
RESOURCES

Number FIVE
Fish and Wildlife Service, United States Department of the Interior, Washington, D. C.

*As a marine biologist and editor for the U.S. Fish and Wildlife Service,
Carson wrote and edited booklets, including this one, about National
Wildlife Refuges.*

and she had high standards for the work produced in her office. But along with her professionalism, Carson had a lighter side. Called "Ray" by her coworkers, she was well-liked and enjoyed office camaraderie. In 1945, Shirley Briggs, a young illustrator, began working in Carson's department. Briggs and Carson collaborated on several projects and became good friends. Briggs later recalled how Carson's "qualities of zest and humor made even the dull stretches of bureaucratic procedure a matter for quiet fun."[2] Office friendships extended beyond work and Carson and her colleagues frequently met for parties and social events. Both bird-watchers, Carson and Briggs went on excursions to Maryland's coast to see shorebirds and to Pennsylvania's mountains to watch migrating hawks. At this time, Carson's home life was less tumultuous than in her first years at work. Her nieces were young women and increasingly on their own. Her mother, as always, lived with her and kept the household running.

An especially enjoyable government project for Carson began just after World War II ended. Starting in 1946, she was responsible for a series of twelve "Conservation in Action" booklets about national wildlife refuges. The refuges are government-owned lands that provide habitat for fish and wildlife. Many refuges are on flyways, routes followed by migrating birds. In the introduction to the booklets, Carson wrote, "for all the people, the preservation of wildlife and of wildlife habitat means also the preservation of the basic resources of the earth, which men, as well as animals, must have in order to live. Wildlife, water, forests, grasslands—all are parts of man's essential environment; the conservation and effective use of one is impossible except as the others also are conserved." The series was clearly ecological, illuminating connections between living things and their environments.[3]

Writing the "Conservation in Action" series required Carson and other biologists to visit national wildlife refuges around the United States. Shirley Briggs illustrated several of the booklets and accompanied Carson on some of these pleasant assignments. At the seaside in Chincoteague, Virginia, the two women went boating and wading with the refuge manager as they learned about oyster beds and clam harvests. The trip also gave them the opportunity to observe skimmers, terns, and other shorebirds that made the refuge their home.

During the summer of 1946 Carson took a much deserved vacation. With her mother and two cats, she went to Maine. She rented a cottage on the water for a month. From the moment they arrived, Carson was enchanted. She explored tidepools, bird-watched, sun-bathed, and visited lobstermen. She was delighted by the calls of ocean birds and the sounds of splashing waves and bells ringing on buoys. In an enthusiastic letter, Carson confided to Briggs that she dreamed of someday owning a cottage there.[4]

Almost immediately after her refreshing month in Maine, Carson was planning an ambitious new book, a natural history of the ocean. During World War II, scientists had gained vast new knowledge about the sea. With ships and submarines sailing to all corners of the globe, understanding tides and ocean currents had been vital to the U. S. Navy. New technologies had revealed underwater landscapes of mountains and canyons that were previously unknown.

In studying the seas for the war effort, a world of oceanographic discoveries were made. Many of

*Carson spent a month in Maine during the summer of 1946. She fell in love with the Maine coast and eventually bought land and built her own cottage there.*

these discoveries were recorded in technical and scientific government reports. Carson was skilled at reading these kinds of reports. She also had a talent for making science interesting for the general public. That fall, Carson threw herself into her new project.

While working on her book, Carson hired a literary agent named Marie Rodell to help her get it published. Bright, energetic, and hardworking, Rodell handled the business end of the book, allowing Carson to concentrate on research and writing. Rodell became a valued friend and assisted Carson with literary projects for the rest of her life. As she researched and wrote, Carson continued her demanding government job. The job gave her a steady paycheck, which she needed since she could not support herself and her mother just with writing.

In 1949, on a government business trip to Florida to visit wildlife areas, Carson had an opportunity to experience the underwater world. Carson had been invited by a professor at the Miami Marine Laboratory to go diving. Scuba diving equipment, invented during World War II, was still not widely available. For Carson to see the depths, she used an old-style eighty-four pound diving helmet and breathed through an air hose that ran to the surface. As she descended from the ladder of the dive boat she felt her ears pop under increasing water pressure. Underwater at last, she stood on the coral shoal and felt the pull of the flowing current. Through the helmet's foggy lens she could see swimming fish, sea fans, and the surface of the sea above her. Carson's only diving experience made a lasting impression on her.

Right after her trip to Florida, Carson combined her government work and book research on a ten-day seafaring expedition. The *Albatross III* was a Fish and Wildlife Service ship based in Woods Hole. The vessel was used for deep-sea research. Carson had arranged to accompany the research crew on a trip to Georges Bank, an important fishing ground about 150 miles from Cape Cod. Spending ten days and nights on the ship, she experienced the constant movement of the open sea, life without land in sight, starry nights, and foggy mornings. She watched the crew haul in great cone-shaped fishing nets that they had dragged 600 feet below them. Cod, goosefish, anglerfish, crabs, starfish, sponges, and other creatures tumbled out of the nets.[5] Carson was amazed by the abundance and variety of life that lived in the depths. Carson wrote about her shipboard observations in a chapter titled "Wind, Sun, and the Spinning of the Earth."

Carson spent three years writing *The Sea Around Us*. She gathered all the latest knowledge about the oceans. Then she slowly and thoughtfully wrote about it. *The Sea Around Us* was published in July

*While working for the government and writing* The Sea Around Us, *Carson spent ten days and nights at sea on this U.S. Fish and Wildlife Service ship, the* Albatross III.

1951. Carson's science was accurate and her words were poetic. Readers were captivated.

*The Sea Around Us* was like a biography of the ocean. The ocean was the book's main character. Carson explained theories about the beginning of the seas. She told about geology and early life forms that emerged in the waters. She wrote of the landscape of slopes and canyons of the ocean floor.

Explaining the tides, she discussed the gravitational pull of the sun and moon on Earth's water. She wrote about Nova Scotia's tides that rise as much as fifty feet and Tahiti's high tide that is barely a foot above low tide. In her chapter "The Birth of an Island," Carson beautifully described volcanoes erupting beneath the sea, spewing hot magma into cold waters.

Carson also wrote about tsunamis—the seismic sea waves caused by underwater earthquakes. She included accounts of the 1946 tsunami that struck Hawaii but was caused by an earthquake 2,000 miles away. She suggested that since these natural events were better understood than ever before, there could be warning systems to alert people on coasts before tsunamis struck.[6]

The critics praised *The Sea Around Us*. The popular book quickly made the bestseller lists, where it remained for more than a year and a half. Carson was honored with prestigious literary awards, including the National Book Award. The Pennsylvania College for Women and other universities awarded her honorary doctorates for her splendid achievement.

As her new book triumphed, *Under the Sea Wind* was re-released. It, too, charged up the bestseller lists, getting the attention that it had missed with the outbreak of war. It must have been a great joy to Carson to finally see her lovely first book read and acclaimed.

The extraordinary success of her books dramatically changed Carson's life. From the money she earned, she could afford to leave her job at the Fish and Wildlife Service and devote herself to her writing full-time. Her success also allowed her to fulfill her dream of owning a cottage on the coast of Maine. Carson purchased a little piece of land on Southport Island and built a cottage between the water and the spruce forest. From her front door she could climb over the rocks to the sea. In 1953, Carson and her mother spent their first summer there. She would return there every summer for the rest of her life.

Carson's niece, Marjorie, and her baby boy, Roger, visited her that first year. One morning during low tide Marjorie and Carson found a large starfish in a tide pool. They carried it to the cottage to show Roger and take his picture with it. While they were at the house, the tide had rolled in. With the high water, the tide pool was submerged. Carson could not take the starfish back to its home. She kept the creature in a pail of saltwater through the day.

*After Carson finished writing* The Sea Around Us, *she began work on her next book,* The Edge of the Sea. *In 1952 she spent time in the Florida Keys observing and studying coral reefs and the creatures that live in them.*

That night, when the tide was low again, she set out with a flashlight. She carried the starfish back to its tide pool, where it belonged.[7]

In her new life, Carson was finally free to write. She wasted no time in starting another sea book. Carson's third book, *The Edge of the Sea*, explored life in different Atlantic coastal environments. The chapter "Rocky Shores" revealed the periwinkles, barnacles, limpets, and other creatures and plants of the northern Atlantic coast, including the coast of Maine.

In the chapter "The Rim of Sand," Carson wrote about the jellyfish, sponges, whelk, and abundant crabs in the waters of the mid-Atlantic states. In "The Coral Coast" chapter, she looked at the extraordinary world of the Florida Keys. With her clear, well-balanced style, she told of the tiny coral polyps that build the reefs, and the barracuda, angelfish, and spiny urchins that inhabit them. Once again, her science and poetry were combined in a single voice.

*The Edge of the Sea*, published in 1955, earned Carson even more awards. For twenty weeks it stayed on bestseller lists around the world.

Famous and internationally respected, Carson was free to pursue her many interests. She wrote a script for a television program about clouds. She wrote a magazine article, "Help Your Child to Wonder," sharing some of the joy she found introducing her nephew, Roger, to the natural world. Learning names and labels was not so important, she stressed, as using your senses to be receptive to the natural world. She wrote of taking Roger out to watch the sea waves in a storm and to observe tiny crabs on the beach at night. She told about their explorations of the Maine woods, walking on rain-soaked lichens and imagining spruce seedlings as Christmas trees for forest creatures. "Help Your Child to Wonder" recalled the nature-study philosophy that Maria Carson had shared with a young Rachel back in Springdale. Carson was considering expanding the article into a book when her life took an unexpected turn.

# The Age of Pesticides

RACHEL CARSON DID NOT GROW UP IN A world of pesticides. The word pesticide was not even in dictionaries when she was a child. Pesticide is derived from two Latin words—*pestis* meaning plague, and *cidu* meaning to kill. Pesticides are chemicals used to kill anything considered to be a pest, like insects or weeds.

The history of modern pesticides began quietly. In 1874 a German chemist produced a man-made chemical called dichloro-diphenyl-trichloroethane. The substance attracted little notice for many years. In 1939, Paul Muller, a chemist, was working in a laboratory at a big chemical company in Switzerland. Muller was looking for chemicals that killed insects that attacked certain plants. In his research, he tried hundreds of different substances. When Muller tested dichloro-diphenyl-trichloroethane, now known as DDT, he observed astonishing results. DDT killed flies, beetles, and many other kinds of insects. Muller also discovered that DDT was persistent. Many hours or even days after it was applied, DDT killed insects that came into contact with it.[1]

When Muller made his discovery, Europe was engulfed in World War II. In 1941, the United States entered the war to fight on the side of the Allies—countries including Great Britain, France, and the Soviet Union. Besides combat, armies encountered other problems. Diseases like typhus and malaria were killing thousands of soldiers and civilians. The typhus bacteria is carried by lice. Malaria is spread by mosquitoes.

The U. S. military was looking for chemicals to kill disease-carrying lice just when a government laboratory received a packet of DDT from Switzerland. Experiments quickly confirmed that body lice, mosquitoes, bedbugs, and many other insects died when exposed to DDT.[2] Almost immediately, the government put DDT to work. In early 1944, a typhus epidemic broke out in Naples,

Italy. The United States military dusted more than one million people there with DDT powder. Within three weeks of the dusting, the people were lice-free and the epidemic was over.[3] For the rest of the war, DDT powder was widely used in Europe and North Africa. It was hailed as a boon to public health. Because it also killed mosquitoes, DDT was used to control malaria, too. DDT seemed like a miracle. Muller won the prestigious Nobel Prize for Medicine for his discovery of DDT's usefulness.

At first, DDT was rationed only for military use. But word spread quickly about this amazing new pesticide. Farmers could see great potential for the chemical. Corn-borers, boll weevils, and other pests reduced the amount and the quality of many agricultural crops. Before World War II, there had been some substances farmers could use against insects, but these were expensive and did not last long. Arsenic and lead were ingredients in prewar insect-killers, and both had serious health risks to humans. DDT, by contrast, killed many kinds of insects and was inexpensive to produce. Because it was persistent, it did not need to be applied too frequently to be effective. It also seemed to be safe.[4]

Not only farmers were excited about DDT. Many

*The pesticide dichloro-diphenyl-trichloroethane (DDT) at first seemed like a miracle chemical. It was very effective at killing many kinds of insects, including disease-carrying lice and mosquitoes. Here a woman in Linz, Austria, is dusted with DDT powder to kill lice in 1945.*

Americans were optimistic that DDT would conquer nuisances like flies and mosquitoes. During the summer of 1945, a Long Island beach in New York was sprayed with fog containing DDT. "In half an hour every insect on the beach was dead," reported *Time* magazine, announcing the experiment's success.[5] After spraying at a resort in Michigan, people celebrated by burning their flytraps in a public bonfire.[6]

In 1945, the U. S. government allowed DDT to be sold to the public. The public was eager to buy. Cheerful advertising campaigns from chemical companies  spread news of the chemical's benefits. Household DDT aerosols were sold. One company even made a science kit for families to experiment with DDT.[7]

As early as 1945, Carson was concerned that DDT was not an unqualified miracle. Carson understood food chains and interactions between living things and their environments. She knew that disruptions to nature could have unintended consequences. She also knew that Elmer Higgins, her former boss, was working with another respected wildlife biologist, to learn more about DDT. Higgins and Clarence Cottam, among others, were studying how the new pesticide affected fish and wildlife. In July 1945, Carson offered to write an article about DDT for *Reader's Digest* magazine. She planned to write about DDT's effects on insects and birds and the balance of nature.[8] The magazine did not want her story.

From the beginning of the modern pesticide era,

there were questions about the safety of these new chemicals. In 1945, *Time* magazine reported the story of a laboratory worker who covered his hands with DDT. While his skin showed no damage, within a few days his arms and legs began to ache. He suffered painful spasms. A year later his health was still not fully restored.[9] The cumulative effects of DDT concerned public health officials. Tests showed that the chemical accumulated in the fat and organs of animals. The long-term effect of this accumulation in animals or humans was unknown. Because disastrous health consequences only seemed to result from large doses and long-term dangers seemed vague, there was a general acceptance that, with "proper use," pesticides were safe.[10]

The use of pesticides expanded quickly. Pesticide companies developed more and more new chemicals. Dieldrin, aldrin, heptachlor, and others were many times stronger than DDT. The business of making and selling pesticides exploded. Some chemical companies rapidly made fortunes in the new business.

There were many levels of use of the new pesticides. Families bought small amounts to spray their vegetable gardens or apple trees. Farmers bought pesticides to spray fields where they grew cotton, corn, wheat, and other crops. The U. S. Department of Agriculture, state governments and local communities also started pesticide spraying programs. The government programs were intended to be for the good of the public. Mosquitoes, gypsy moths, tent caterpillars, spruce budworms, and fire ants were all targets of government campaigns. Some programs covered huge areas, drenching fields and forests with chemicals sprayed from airplanes. Mosquito trucks drove through towns fogging neighborhoods with pesticide mist. In many of these programs, property owners were not consulted. Their land was sprayed whether they wanted to be included or not.

By the late 1950s, people who lived in places that were sprayed began to be alarmed. While many government officials and chemical company representatives claimed that the spraying was safe, people often saw much death after pesticide use. Concerned citizens began to protest.

Olga Owens Huckins, who lived in Duxbury, Massachusetts, wrote an outraged letter to the editor of the *Boston Herald* newspaper in January 1958. As part of a Massachusetts pesticide program to control

*A pesticide spraying program in a coastal area of Duxbury, Massachusetts killed songbirds and outraged property owners.*

mosquitoes in nearby marshes, Huckins' land was sprayed repeatedly from an airplane in the summer of 1957. Immediately after the spraying, Huckins began to find bodies of songbirds. She found dead birds at her door, by the birdbath, and falling from trees. "All of these birds died horribly, and in the same way. Their bills were gaping open and their splayed claws were drawn up to their breasts in agony." These symptoms were known to result from large doses of pesticides. "Air spraying where it is not needed or wanted is inhuman, undemocratic, and probably unconstitutional," Huckins wrote. "For those of us who stand helplessly on the tortured earth, it is intolerable."[11] Huckins sent a copy of her letter to Rachel Carson.

At about the same time that Carson read Huckins' letter, she learned about a court case regarding pesticides. During the summer of 1957, several New York communities were sprayed in a government program intended to control gypsy moths. Property owners were not asked whether their land could be sprayed. Marjorie Spock and Mary Richards had a large organic vegetable garden at their home. For health reasons, they had carefully kept their garden free of chemicals. Yet, due to the gypsy moth spraying program, their garden was doused over and over by low-flying pesticide airplanes.[12] Richards, Spock, and other community members brought a lawsuit against the U. S. Department of Agriculture to stop spraying their land.

At the time the lawsuit was initiated and Huckins was writing to the newspaper, Carson was taking on new family responsibilities. She had been very fond of her niece Marjorie. In 1957, Marjorie died and

*To kill malaria-carrying mosquitoes, DDT was mixed with oil and sprayed from airplanes over mosquito breeding grounds. Here, an army barracks in Arkansas is sprayed with DDT.*

Carson stepped in to raise her son, Roger Christie. Carson and her ninety-year-old mother adjusted their home life to include the six-year-old.

Carson believed that it was vital that the problems of pesticides be exposed, but it was a bad time for her to take on a new project. However, with the urging of a fellow writer and with interest from *The New Yorker* magazine, Carson decided to tackle the issue herself. *The New Yorker* already had published excerpts of Carson's *The Sea Around Us* and *The Edge of the Sea*.

Carson threw herself into the monumental task of researching pesticides. Spock and Richards kept her apprised of events in the court case. In the meantime, Carson gathered wildlife studies and reports about government spraying programs. She soon recognized that the magazine piece would be part of a larger book.

Learning about pesticides dominated Carson's life. Even at her cottage in Maine with her mother and Roger, she worked on her research. She read reports by John George, a wildlife biologist. George had documented how DDT killed fish and animals in a spraying program in New York. She learned about George Wallace, a scientist who specialized in the study of birds. Wallace had seen the effects of DDT on robins in Michigan. Carson contacted scientists knowledgeable about soils and groundwater. Her research brought her back in touch with wildlife biologist Clarence Cottam. He knew a great deal about a massive government spraying program that was targeting fire ants.

In December 1958, Rachel Carson's beloved mother, Maria, died. Mother and daughter had

# D D T

*(Dichloro)*     *(Diphenyl)*     *(Trichloroethane)*

### *The Famous Wartime Insecticide Discovery*

## Now Available to Civilians

D D T is a powder used as a basic ingredient for various types of insecticides, powdered and liquid. There are various mixtures for different uses:

- Compounded with other powders, for dusting purposes
- Solutions, containing DDT mixed with water
- DDT mixed with other ingredients and volatile solvents, for spraying or brushing

*Prices will vary according to type and quality of the product.*

> *There Will Be Varying Types and Qualities of D D T Sprays. For Your Protection, Get Facts About Each Before You Buy!*

## MADACO DDT Base Insecticide

is a liquid compound of D D T, PYRETHRUM and other ingredients. (CONTAINS NO KEROSENE) making it most effective against household insects. It is to be used as a spray for killing, as well as repelling, all household pests. Used according to directions MADACO DDT BASE INSECTICIDE will kill them promptly and act to repel them for a period of from sixty to ninety days.

| | | | |
|---|---|---|---|
| 55 Gal. Drums, per gal. | **$3.10** | 30 Gal. Drums, per gal. | **$3.25** |
| 5 Gallon Containers, per gal. | **$3.50** | 2 Gallon Containers, per gal. | **$3.75** |
| | 1 Gallon Containers, per gal. | **$3.85** | |

Out-of-town shipments prepaid on orders of five (5) gallons or over. Check or money order must accompany one and two gallon mail orders. Deliveries will be made promptly. Add 25c per gal. to cover shipping charges on one or two gallon orders out of Jacksonville.

### *Proper Precautions Necessary for Best Results*

All containers are labeled with proper instructions and precautions conforming with bulletins issued by the War Food Administration, Offices of Marketing Services, Washington, D. C.

## Marion H. Davis & Co.

**1212 Mary St.**        **Phone 9-6636**

---

*An advertisement in the* Tallahassee Democrat *newspaper announcing DDT sale to the public.*

always been together. Maria Carson had seen Rachel grow from childhood nature-study lessons to become a spokesperson for ecology. Maria had supported her daughter's writing from her early stories about wrens and bunnies through three best-selling books. She was proud of her daughter's achievements. Through many decades, Maria Carson had cooked, cleaned, and managed their home. Rachel Carson truly mourned her mother's passing.

Driven by her concern about pesticides, Carson soon returned to her research. Besides looking at the impact of pesticides on wildlife, she wanted to know how pesticides affected human health. She learned about the work of Otto Warburg, a German biologist. Warburg was studying how certain substances caused cells to change and become cancerous. Another medical researcher, Malcolm Hargraves was exploring connections between pesticides and leukemia.

Carson's book was a huge project. Besides the work the book required, she was raising her nephew Roger. In a cruel twist of fate, poor health complicated her life further. In March 1960, she went to the hospital after detecting unusual lumps in one breast. Ten years earlier she had a breast tumor removed. Back in 1950, it did not seem that she had cancer. This time, though, she had extensive surgery as her doctor removed the cancerous tumors and surrounding tissue. Carson's doctor did not tell her that the growth was malignant.[14] Malignant tumors mean that the cancer is spreading.

After the surgery Carson was weak and often in pain, but she was determined to finish her book. She worked in bed and dictated changes to her manuscript into a tape recorder. Since computers did not exist then, all of Carson's writing was done on a typewriter. During this time an assistant typed for her. By summer, Carson was strong enough to go to Maine. All year she pushed on with the book. In December 1960, Carson learned some crushing news. Her cancer had spread.

The next year, 1961, was even more challenging. While having radiation treatments for her cancer, painful arthritis flared up. Carson wrote when she could. She and Roger and the cats went to Maine for part of the summer. In the fall she endured more cancer treatments while reviewing illustrations and making final changes to her book. At last, as 1962 opened, her work was done. Chapters of *Silent Spring* would appear in *The New Yorker* first, followed by the complete book.

# Silent Spring

RACHEL CARSON'S *SILENT SPRING* ALERTED readers to humankind's capacity to destroy the environment and endanger human health. A powerful book with a compelling message, it opened gently. "There was once a town in the heart of America where all life seemed to live in harmony with its surroundings," wrote Carson.[1] The first chapter is called "A Fable for Tomorrow." She described a healthy town, a bit like the Springdale of her youth. Hillside orchards blossomed in the springtime. Wildflowers grew by the roads. Foxes and deer were at home there. Flocks of migrating birds traveled through the town in spring and fall.

"Then a strange blight crept over the area and everything began to change," Carson wrote.[2] Farm

animals died. Adults and children fell ill with unknown sicknesses. Plants by the roadsides perished. No fish swam in the streams. "On the mornings that had once throbbed with the dawn chorus of robins, catbirds, doves, jays, wrens, and scores of other bird voices there was now no sound; only silence lay over the fields and woods and marsh."[3] How had this death and desolation come to the town? "The people," explained Carson, "had done it themselves."[4]

The town in her fable was fictional but the deaths and disasters Carson described had all actually happened. Their cause, she would show in the following chapters, was pesticide. In *Silent Spring*, Carson presented her warning carefully and persuasively.

A great strength of Carson's writing was her ability to make complicated material interesting and understandable. She succeeded brilliantly in the chapter explaining the chemistry of pesticides. Few nonscientists talked about "chlorinated hydrocarbons" before *Silent Spring*. After reading Carson's lucid explanation they had some understanding of how carbon, hydrogen, and chlorine atoms could be combined into a variety of deadly substances.

Carson explained that chlorinated hydrocarbons

dissolved in fat and oil. Because they dissolved in fats, they accumulated in certain fatty tissues in human beings and animals. She showed how chlorinated hydrocarbons, including DDT, traveled up food chains, becoming more concentrated. Hayfields, she explained, were sometimes sprayed with DDT. A cow that ate the sprayed hay might have 3 parts per million of DDT in her milk. But butter, made from the fat in the cow's milk, could have 65 parts per million of DDT.[5] A person who ate the butter had never been near the sprayed hay but consumed the DDT all the same.

In her book, Carson reviewed many of the U. S. government pesticide spraying programs. She examined programs that targeted fire ants, Japanese beetles, gypsy moths, sandflies, and other insects.

*In the 1950s, DDT was widely used in the United States. This can of DDT for household use sold for 45 cents.*

She told about different chemicals used on fields, farms, marshes, and neighborhoods. Through her meticulous research, Carson had found that some programs had failed miserably. They failed to control the pest problem and they also had horrific side effects. Many pest-control programs had tragic consequences. One program familiar to many Americans was a well-intentioned effort to save elm trees. American elm trees used to grow throughout the eastern United States. The trees stood as tall as 100 feet. With spreading branches that gracefully drooped at the ends, elms were familiar sights in forests, parks, and along streets. In the 1930s, a fungus from Europe accidentally came to the United States. Called Dutch elm disease, the fungus grew in the sap of the trees. Once established in a tree, the fungus usually killed it. Little beetles that lived in elm bark carried the fungus from tree to tree. In the 1950s, elm trees across the country were dying. To stop Dutch elm disease from spreading, communities started spraying elms with DDT to kill the bark beetles.

In 1954, elm trees on the campus of Michigan State University were sprayed with DDT. The following spring, the robins flew in on their annual migration from the south. Shortly after arriving, they began to die. George Wallace, an ornithologist, a scientist who studies birds, taught at the university. At first, Wallace thought the birds were dying from a nervous system disease.[6] He soon realized that they were dying from insecticide poisoning. They had, he explained, "well-known symptoms of loss of balance, followed by tremors, convulsions, and death."[7] What was perplexing, though, was that the robins were not on the campus when the trees were sprayed.

The mystery of the dead robins was soon solved. DDT lasts for a long time. Elm leaves that had been sprayed with DDT had fallen to the ground in the autumn. Earthworms crawled through the leaves and ate them. The worms carried the DDT in their bodies. When the robins returned in the spring, they ate the poisoned worms. Researchers found that eleven toxic worms could kill a robin.[8] The robins on the Michigan campus were dying before they reproduced. Instead of new generations of robins hopping around the college, in the spring of 1958, there were none.[9]

Carson wrote about the decline in bald eagle populations. Across the country in the 1950s, bird-watchers and wildlife biologists saw fewer bald eagles, ospreys, and certain other predatory birds. The failing birds were high on the food chain— eagles and ospreys eat mostly fish. Carson told how surveys of eagle nests in Florida confirmed that young birds were not replacing old ones as they died off. Fewer eagles were nesting, but even when the birds laid eggs, it seemed that few baby eaglets hatched. Carson suggested that DDT was to blame.[10] She explained that the pesticide had been widely sprayed on lakes and marshes to kill mosquito larvae. Fish that survived the spraying carried DDT in their bodies. When eagles and other birds ate the fish, the DDT accumulated in them.

Carson's suggestion that DDT was responsible for the decrease in bird reproduction was later established conclusively. After DDT is in an animal's body it chemically changes to another substance called DDE, or dichloro-diphenyl-dichloroethylene. DDE interferes with the reproduction of eagles and other birds. Researchers found that female birds with too much DDE in their bodies often laid eggs that had thin shells. The chemical also affected the formation of pores, or tiny holes, in the eggshells. When a mother eagle or osprey sat upon thinned eggs, the fragile eggs often broke. The eggshells with no pores suffocated the embryos inside.[11] The embryos died before they hatched.

In *Silent Spring*, Carson wrote about a U. S. Department of Agriculture program to eradicate fire ants. Eradicate means to destroy completely. Carson contended that the need for this program was exaggerated and that it was launched without adequate understanding of the destructiveness of the pesticides that were used.

Like the fungus that causes Dutch elm disease, fire ants are not native to North America. They arrived in this country early in the 1900s and began building their ant hills in the south. Fire ants have a nasty sting that irritates the skin. Their huge ant hills are a nuisance to farmers. The hills, often over a foot and a half tall, interfere with plowing fields and harvesting crops. In researching the fire ant program, Carson learned from government scientists that the ants actually did little damage to plants and livestock. She also learned that the ants eat other insects including boll weevils that are serious agricultural pests.

In the fire ant program, the government used two new pesticides—dieldrin and heptachlor. These were both many times more lethal than DDT. The effect of these chemicals on animals was not known. The minimum quantity needed to kill the ants was not known either.[12] Despite concerns by conservationists, spraying began in 1958.

In the fire ant eradication program, the pesticides were not just applied to the anthills. They were mixed with oil and sprayed from airplanes over vast tracts of land.

Wildlife devastation from the fire ant eradication program was immediate. In one Texas county, small animals including armadillos and raccoons disappeared from the sprayed lands.[13] Songbirds, woodcock, and turkeys died. In Alabama, more than 100 quail were counted on a parcel of land before it was sprayed. After the pesticides were applied, no living quail were left. A pig farmer whose land was sprayed found that his little pigs were born dead or died soon after birth. Farm animals that grazed on the sprayed land or drank water contaminated with pesticide died of a disease of the nervous system.

For five years, twenty million acres of land in the southern United States were sprayed with pesticides intended to kill fire ants. The area sprayed was about as large as the states of Vermont and New Hampshire combined. The program was expensive

*Rachel Carson's book* Silent Spring *alerted readers to the dangers of DDT and other pesticides. Since the ban on DDT, many of these species have made impressive recoveries. These bald eagle chicks are among the birds in these new generations.*

and destructive, and it failed. Fire ants continued to expand their infestation.

In studying the fire ant program and other chemical attacks on pests, Carson found a tragic irony. In spite of the spraying, populations of the target pests often came back. Worse still, the later populations of insects were often resistant to the pesticide. For example, at first DDT had seemed like a miracle in the prevention of typhus fever because it killed lice. Less than ten years later, scientists found that DDT was ineffective in killing lice in many countries where it had previously been used. The lice had become resistant to the chemical. Resistance to DDT was also found in malarial mosquitoes, houseflies, ticks, coddling moths, and sixty other types of insects by 1960.[14]

Carson explained that the rapid reproduction of insects contributed to their ability to become resistant. Many generations of insects are born within a year. When sprayed with pesticides, the weakest ones died. The survivors were left to produce the next generation. The genetic characteristics of the parent insects that made them pesticide-resistant were passed on to their children.

In *Silent Spring,* Carson presented heartbreaking but true stories about wildlife disasters caused by pesticides. She also raised another important issue. People were constantly exposed to pesticides. Pesticides were sprayed directly on some fruits and vegetables that people ate. People drank milk from cows that had consumed pesticides on hay. Chickens ate feed sprayed with pesticides. People ate eggs. People swam in lakes and drank water that contained pesticides.

In explaining how pesticides had poisoned the environment, Carson showed how humankind put itself at risk. Pesticides are almost everywhere on earth now, carried around the planet by water, wind, and living things. People on all continents have some pesticides in their body. Human mother's milk contains traces of pesticides. Pesticides are in the ice in Antarctica.[15]

Carson believed there were links between pesticides and human health. She was concerned that not enough was known about connections between pesticides and diseases including cancer. She knew of tragic cases where farmers exposed to large doses of pesticides were stricken with leukemia, a kind of cancer, and died.[16] One medical expert, Dr. Hargraves, believed that there was a connection between pesticides and this blood disorder. Carson presented the case that it was likely that some pesticides were carcinogens. Carcinogens are substances that cause cancer.

In *Silent Spring*, Carson discussed how chemicals could interfere in reproduction. Fewer birds and baby pigs were born when the parents were exposed to pesticides. What were the risks for human beings? Carson did not pretend to know all the answers to these health questions. She made a compelling case that there was evidence that pesticides harmed human health. She showed that it was not clear that there were safe levels of exposure. She alerted readers that combinations of chemicals could cause effects different than those produced by the individual substances.

Carson ended her book on a hopeful note. The final chapter was called "The Other Road." Throughout the book, she had shown how people had chosen to follow the path of using DDT and related chlorinated hydrocarbon pesticides to solve insect problems. People could turn away from that destructive path, she suggested. Individuals, government, and businesses could reduce their use of these pesticides. She wrote about tests and encouraging studies using alternatives to chemicals, especially biological controls to reduce insect populations. Biological controls involve using the natural enemies of pests. In conclusion, she urged readers to recognize that we share the earth with many living things. Rather than trying to control nature, we should cautiously seek solutions that accommodate insects and other diverse life, not just humankind.[17]

# 8

# "Noisy Summer"

CARSON EXPECTED *SILENT SPRING* TO BE controversial. Her words carried a strong warning about the dangers of pesticides. She exposed irresponsible actions of chemical companies and the government in using pesticides without understanding their risks. If people heeded Carson's warning, changes in the business and government practices would have to occur.

On June 16, 1962, the first of three excerpts from *Silent Spring* was published in *The New Yorker* magazine. The controversy produced was fierce. Supporters applauded Carson's courage. The American public had seen neighborhood fogging and government spraying programs and many

people had wondered about safety. Readers enthusiastically read Carson's words to learn more. At the same time, chemical companies began attacking Carson and her views.

"'*Silent Spring*' is now Noisy Summer," read a *New York Times* headline on July 22. The subheads read "Pesticides Industry Up in Arms Over a New Book" and "Rachel Carson Stirs Conflict—Producers are Crying Foul."[1] *The New York Times* article reported the pesticide producers' indignation over Carson's book, which was due to be released in the fall. Industry spokesmen did not dispute her facts, but they said that she ignored the benefits of pesticides. One chemical company spokesman charged that Carson was "a fanatic defender of the cult of the balance of nature."[2]

For a little peace, Carson went to her beloved cottage. Roger and her cats went with her. In Maine, Carson enjoyed the quiet company of friends. Tidepools, fragrant spruce trees, and seaside birds would help her conserve her strength for the storm of attention that would accompany the book's September release.

Carson was in Maine when a representative of the Velsicol Chemical Company of Chicago tried to

*Rachel Carson on the deck of her summer home in Maine in 1961.*

convince her publisher not to release the book. He hinted that Carson might be part of a foreign plot to deprive Americans of their abundant food supply.[3] The National Agricultural Chemicals Association (NACA) also launched attacks on Carson. NACA would spend more than $250,000 trying to refute Carson's case.

Carson's supporters spoke out. William O. Douglas, a United States Supreme Court Justice, wrote a review of *Silent Spring*. Douglas compared Carson's book to another powerful book, Harriet Beecher Stowe's *Uncle Tom's Cabin*. In 1852, Stowe vividly portrayed the inhumanity of human slavery. After reading her story, many readers felt strongly that slavery should be outlawed. Abolition of slavery became one of the central issues in the American Civil War. Douglas declared *Silent Spring* one of the most important books of the century. He saw it as a call to action to control the use of pesticides.[4]

*Silent Spring* immediately attracted government attention. Through the Department of Agriculture, the United States was organizing and paying for pesticide spraying. At the same time, the Fish and Wildlife Service had evidence that spraying programs had harmful effects. As word of *Silent*

*Spring*'s warning spread, President John F. Kennedy appointed a special advisory committee to look at issues of pesticide use.

The negative reaction to *Silent Spring* escalated when the book was released in September 1962. Monsanto, a chemical manufacturer, published a satire of *Silent Spring*. They called it "The Desolate Year." It portrayed life without pesticides as barely worth living. The National Pest Control Association developed an information packet criticizing Carson. It included a poem sung to the tune of the folk song "Rubin, Rubin." One verse read "Hunger, hunger, are you listening, To the words from Rachel's pen? Words which taken at face value, Place lives of birds 'bove those of men."[5]

The attacks on Carson took several forms. Many portrayed her as opposed to all pesticide use. This was untrue. Carson did not say that pesticides should never be used, but she did warn that they were being handled by people who did not understand their capacity to do harm.[6] She cautioned that their use should be limited and they should be used carefully. Some belittled her as a hysterical woman who loved birds more than people. Others tried to question her credentials as a scientist.

Thousands of readers all over the country and around the world bought *Silent Spring*. The book soared to the top of bestseller lists. People quickly understood Carson's warning. They were disturbed about the abuse of nature and risks to human health. Carson received many fan letters. One New York reader wrote, "As I drive home along the Hudson tonight I'll feel more human for having read your lovely, loving words today. I know, too, that your great quiet eloquence will open many eyes and close many bottles."[7]

Carson's celebrity grew. Eric Severeid of CBS Television interviewed Carson for a special news program called "The *Silent Spring* of Rachel Carson." In the television program, she read passages from her book. She laid out the facts about the hazards and failures of pesticides. Dr. Robert White-Stevens, representing the chemical companies, was also interviewed. White-Stevens came across as loud and alarmist.[8] The program was a triumph for Carson. Many newspaper cartoons featured Carson and *Silent Spring*. Her name was in Charles Schulz's comic strip, "Peanuts," three times. Children learned that Carson was a famous and influential woman.

As 1963 dawned, Carson began receiving honors and prestigious awards for *Silent Spring*. Tragically, her health was rapidly deteriorating. Pain and weakness made it impossible for her to attend many award ceremonies. One honor she valued highly was the Schweitzer Medal from the Animal Welfare Institute, and she made the trip to New York in order to receive it. The medal honored her "contribution to the protection of animals from damage from pesticides such as DDT."[9] Carson had long admired Dr. Albert Schweitzer, a physician, writer, missionary, and philosopher who taught a "reverence for life," and was renowned for his work in Africa.

Other awards followed. The National Wildlife Federation honored Carson as Conservationist of the Year. The National Audubon Society and American Geographical Society both awarded her medals for her achievement.

President Kennedy's Science Advisory Committee gathered information about pesticides and met with Carson. These advisers reviewed government programs and interviewed experts. In May 1963, when the committee released its report, it endorsed Carson's warning. It criticized the chemical industry

*United States Secretary of the Interior Stuart Udall presents an award to Rachel Carson in 1962.*

and government agencies. Like later government reports, it recommended phasing out DDT and certain other pesticides. The report acknowledged Carson's contribution in alerting the public to "the toxicity of pesticides."[10]

The day after the report was released, the U. S. Senate began hearings on environmental hazards. When Carson testified before the committee a few weeks later, she made clear recommendations. Carson said that pesticide spraying programs should be strictly controlled. She urged that a committed effort begin to eventually eliminate long-lasting, persistent pesticides.[11]

Between the government's response and readers' enthusiasm, Carson could see that her message was heard. She saw hopeful signs that the negligent use of pesticides would change. At the same time, her health was failing.

Carson's cancer had spread. She had also developed a heart condition. At times she was in great pain. At other times she was nauseated from treatments. She spent several quiet summer weeks at her cottage. Walking was difficult for her and she was often in a wheelchair.

During the fall of 1963, Carson summoned her

strength for a trip to California. In San Francisco she delivered a speech on "The Pollution of the Environment." She spoke of herself as an ecologist and talked about the interdependence of life and the environment.[12]

Despite her failing health, Carson was no doubt pleased with the way things were going. People everywhere were becoming much more aware of the environment.

# "A Tide of Environmental Consciousness"

"THE GENERAL USE OF THE PESTICIDE DDT will no longer be legal in the United States after today," began a U. S. government press release issued on December 31, 1972.[1] Ten years after Carson alerted the world to the health and environmental dangers from pesticides, DDT was banned in the United States. Sadly, Carson did not live to see this landmark environmental decision.

Controversy, attacks, honors, and acclaim for Carson followed the publication of *Silent Spring*. Carson's cancer kept progressing and she was very weak. In early 1964, she rewrote her will. She decided to leave her manuscripts, notes, letters, and other papers to Yale University. She arranged for the financial support of her nephew Roger. She finalized bequests for friends, relatives, and two environmental organizations, The Nature Conservancy and The Sierra Club.[2]

Rachel Carson died that spring. She passed away on April 14, 1964, at her home in Silver Spring, Maryland. Friends, colleagues, and relatives mourned Carson's passing. News of her death saddened countless others who had never met her but had been moved by her words.

Rachel Carson left a legacy of literature and environmental awareness. Because of her writing, people began to change their views of nature and humankind's responsibility to the environment. By skillfully presenting scientific facts in clear poetic language, Carson shared her lifelong love of nature with her readers. She inspired an ecological view of the world.

Before she died, Carson had the satisfaction of knowing that her words had moved and influenced many people. Her best-selling sea books gave readers new appreciation of the oceans. Describing the birth of islands, underwater landscapes, and the constantly flowing ocean waters, *The Sea Around Us* offered insights into the sea's natural history. *The Edge of the Sea* and *Under the Sea Wind* both illuminated the intricate webs of life and connections between creatures and the ocean environment.

Carson lived to see that *Silent Spring*'s warning about the reckless use of pesticides was heard. She did not live long enough to see how far-reaching the book's influence would be. She did not know that her book energized a powerful new environmental movement.

After *Silent Spring*'s publication, citizens around the nation and the world increasingly called for environmental responsibility. Individuals banded together to form groups that demanded protection of the earth's air, land, and water. Their demands spurred changes in U. S. laws. They led to international treaties to control pollutants.

In 1970, in response to the public's demands, the United States took a major step toward caring for the environment. Congress created the Environmental Protection Agency (EPA). The EPA's mission is to protect human health and the environment. The agency oversees fifteen different federal programs dealing with pollution. These include the Clean Air Act and the Clean Water Act, both first passed in 1972. Chemicals emitted from factory smokestacks and automobiles are among the pollutants regulated under the Clean Air Act. The Clean Water Act regulates chemicals that go into the nation's lakes, rivers, bays, and coastal waters. Waste from household toilets, chemical discharges from factories, and pesticides and fertilizers that run off of agricultural fields are among the problems addressed by this legislation. Many rivers and lakes are now healthier, some are even safe for swimming, because of the Clean Water Act.

Environmental laws in the United States can be credited with many improvements in the quality of our country's water, air, and soil during the last few decades. However, the population of the country and our world has grown. Demands on natural resources and the environment are greater than ever before. There are more chemicals and more pollutants today than when Rachel Carson wrote *Silent Spring*. Continued pesticide use remains on today's long list of environmental concerns.

The issues that Rachel Carson raised in *Silent Spring* are still debated. DDT and certain other pesticides are no longer permitted in the United

States. However, millions of tons of new pesticides are used here each year. Some of these are chemically related to DDT. The EPA regulates pesticides that may be manufactured and used in the United States. It sets limits on how they may be applied. Pesticides are required to be tested to evaluate their safety. Pesticide registration, explains the EPA, "assures that pesticides will be properly labeled and that if in accordance with specifications, will not cause unreasonable harm to the environment."[3]

Controversies surrounding pesticide use endure. People have differing views of what is "unreasonable harm to the environment." Questions about human health risks persist too. Certain pesticides are banned in European countries because they are considered unsafe. Some of those banned pesticides are still allowed to be used in the United States. Environmentalists, including former Vice President Al Gore, question whether our government's standards are sufficient.[4] Today, the American public is exposed to a wide variety of chemicals. One pesticide may be sprayed on grapes, another on potatoes, and still another on lettuce. One person may consume tiny amounts of several pesticides in a single meal.

Internationally, there are still other pesticide problems. Some pesticides, including DDT, are illegal in the United States but are used elsewhere. The people and environment in those countries remain exposed to these chemicals. When we import food from those nations, these substances still enter the United States.

Many countries are trying to work together to address pesticide problems. In 2001, the United Nations sponsored the Stockholm Convention on Persistent Organic Pollutants. The United States and other countries who sign this treaty agree to reduce or eliminate the production and use of twelve pollutants. These persistent organic pollutants, called POPs, are toxic, last a long time in the environment, and bioaccumulate. Bioaccumulation is when substances accumulate in greater densities as they travel up the food chain, as DDT did with eagles. POPs are linked to problems in human health and animals. The treaty targets twelve substances as the "dirty dozen." These include some of the same pesticides Rachel Carson warned about—DDT, aldrin, chlordane, dieldrin, endrin, and heptachlor.

Since Carson's death, her important contributions to the environment have been honored by the U. S. government. In 1980, President Jimmy Carter awarded Rachel Carson the Presidential Medal of Freedom. Her citation read, "A biologist with a gentle, clear gentle voice, she welcomed her

*The Rachel Carson National Wildlife Refuge in Maine provides important feeding and breeding ground for many species of migratory and shore birds. The refuge was established in 1966 and was renamed to honor Rachel Carson in 1969.*

audiences to her love of the sea, while with an equally clear determined voice, she warned Americans of the dangers human beings themselves pose for their own environment. Always concerned, always eloquent, she created a tide of environmental consciousness that has not ebbed."[5] The Fish and Wildlife Service, her former employer, named the Rachel Carson National Wildlife Refuge in her honor. The refuge includes miles of lands in salt marshes and river estuaries along the coast of Maine. It provides valuable habitat for shorebirds, waterfowl, songbirds, and other wildlife.

Today, bald eagles, ospreys, and other bird populations that suffered from pesticides are recovering. In 1963, the year after *Silent Spring* was published, a survey estimated that there were only 417 nesting pairs of bald eagles in the continental United States. With problems of eggshell thinning and reproductive failure caused by pesticides, the survival of future generations was far from certain. Even after the ban on DDT went into effect in 1972, few eaglets hatched. The persistent residue from the pesticide was still lethal.

Slowly, in the early 1980s, the eagles began to rebound. More eaglets hatched, survived, and matured to start new generations. In 2000, the U. S. Fish and Wildlife Service estimated there were 5,748 nesting pairs of bald eagles in the lower forty-eight states.[6] Back from the brink of extinction, bald eagles are now listed as a threatened rather than an endangered species in many states.

After several springs without the cheery songs of young robins, change came to Michigan State University. In the 1960s, DDT use was stopped. Every year adult robins arrived on campus with the first breath of warm air. But without the pesticide, more birds survived to nest, lay eggs, and care for their young. In 1979, young robins were leaving their nests and setting out on their own in the same numbers as before DDT was ever used.[7]

The spring chorus of birdsong at Michigan State University, near bald eagle nests, and around the country is part of the legacy of Rachel Carson.

# Activities

**Activity 1**

Carson once wrote an article called "Help Your Child to Wonder." It was published in *Women's Home Companion* magazine in 1956. After Carson died, the article was published as a book titled *The Sense of Wonder*.

Carson had a lifelong love of the natural world. In the "Wonder" article and book Carson wrote of happy experiences she shared with Roger, her nephew. They looked at shells, walked in the rain, and listened to insects and the wind together. Carson wrote that she wished it was possible to give each child in the world an enduring sense of wonder. She offered advice to parents about enjoying nature with children, emphasizing that learning facts about nature was less important  than experiencing it.

You can try some of Carson's suggestions.

Carson suggested going outside at night when the moon is full, in the spring or fall. During the spring many birds migrate north and in the fall they travel south. Carson suggested that you find a quiet comfortable place to sit. Listen to the night sounds. You may hear the calls of migrating birds. Binoculars can help you watch the night-flying flocks.

To enjoy the beauty in natural things, Carson suggested that you look at objects as though you had never seen them before or would never see them again. By using your senses you can see ordinary things in a new way. You can look at a twig, a pebble, a seedling, or a leaf. Give yourself time to think about how it feels or if it smells. You can close your eyes and picture it in your mind. If you have a magnifying glass, you can get a closer look at it. A magnifying glass is especially helpful in looking at the veins of leaves, bark, and the center of flowers.

Carson suggested listening to sounds of insects, songs of birds, thunder, and the wind. In a park or yard, make time to stop and listen to nature's sounds. Listen for different bird's voices—some chirp, others whistle or many coo. Can you hear frogs croaking or insects buzzing? You may hear the rustle of leaves or the running water of a stream or river. Giving yourself enough time to listen and be relaxed is important. Usually, as you start to follow different sounds, you will discover many more than you expected. You will probably hear other sounds, too, including human voices or traffic.

## Activity 2

Carson is considered a founder of the modern environmental movement. Many environmental programs, actions, decisions, and volunteer efforts are going on all the time.

To get an idea of environmental issues in your region and around the world, read a newspaper. Starting on the front page, look through the entire newspaper for articles, advertisements, letters, or cartoons about the environment. Write a list of the things you find. Some may be about international efforts like the treaty on persistent organic pollutants. Others may be about Environmental Protection Agency programs or decisions. You may find articles about global warming, mercury levels in fish, automobiles that run on vegetable oil, or environmental groups in your area. Environmental issues are in the news every day.

## Activity 3

Rachel Carson worked for the Bureau of Fisheries and the Fish and Wildlife Service for fifteen years.

She was responsible for many government publications. One project she particularly enjoyed was a series of booklets about national wildlife refuges. The booklets were called "Conservation in Action." Today, more than 500 refuges are publicly owned and managed to protect wildlife and wildlife habitat. There is a wildlife refuge in every state in the country. Wildlife refuges are open to the public. Many have hiking trails or wildlife viewing stations. You can learn more about refuges and find one near you by visiting the National Wildlife Refuge Web site.

# Chronology

1874—German chemist synthesizes dichloro-diphenyl-trichloroethane, later known as DDT.

1907—May 27, Rachel Carson is born to Maria McLean and Robert Carson in Springdale, Pennsylvania.

1918—Children's magazine *St. Nicholas for Boys and Girls* publishes Carson's story, "A Battle in the Clouds."

1925—Graduates from Parnassus High School with highest grades in her class.

1929—Graduates from Pennsylvania College for Women. Spends summer as a beginning investigator at Woods Hole Marine Biological Laboratory. Begins graduate school at Johns Hopkins University in Baltimore.

1930—Carson's family leaves Springdale to live with her near Baltimore.

1932—Receives Master's degree in zoology from Johns Hopkins University. Works part-time teaching biology at University of Maryland.

1935—Father dies. Carson takes civil service examination to apply to work as a government biologist. Works part-time for Bureau of Fisheries writing radio scripts.

1936—Begins career at Bureau of Fisheries as wildlife biologist. Writes articles for *Baltimore Sun* newspaper.

1937—*Atlantic Monthly* publishes Carson's article "Undersea."

1939—Swiss chemist Paul Muller discovers effectiveness of dichloro-diphenyl-trichloroethane (DDT) for killing insects.

1941—Publishes first book, *Under the Sea Wind*.

1945—Proposes writing article about studies assessing DDT's impact on insects, birds, and wildlife.

1946—Works as assistant to chief of Office of Information of U. S. Fish and Wildlife Service. Begins "Conservation in Action" series about national wildlife refuges.

1951—Publishes *The Sea Around Us*.

1952—Wins National Book Award and other honors. *Under the Sea Wind* is reissued. Retires from Fish and Wildlife Service.

1953—Buys land and builds cottage on the coast of Maine.

1955—Publishes *The Edge of the Sea*.

1956—*Woman's Home Companion* magazine publishes Carson's article "Help Your Child to Wonder."

1958—Carson begins researching pesticide use. Maria McLean Carson dies.

1960—Learns she has cancer.

1962—*Silent Spring* is published. President John F. Kennedy's Science Advisory Committee begins study of pesticide use.

1963—Carson honored by National Wildlife Federation, American Academy of Arts and Sciences, Audubon Society, and many other prominent organizations. U. S. Senate begins hearings on hazardous substance use.

1964—Dies on April 14, at age fifty-six.

1970—U. S. Fish and Wildlife Service dedicates the Rachel Carson National Wildlife Refuge in Maine in Carson's honor. Environmental Protection Agency is established.

1972—Use of dichloro-diphenyl-trichloroethane, DDT, is banned in the United States.

# Chapter Notes

## Chapter 1. Deadly Consequences

1. George J. Wallace, "Insecticides and Birds," *Audubon Magazine*, vol. 61, no. 1, January-February 1959, p. 10.

2. Ibid., p. 11.

3. Walter Rosene, "Effects of Field Applications of Heptachlor on Bobwhite Quail and Other Wild Animals," *Journal of Wildlife Management*, vol. 29, no. 3, July 1965, pp. 571–572.

4. Rachel Carson, *Silent Spring* (Boston: Houghton Mifflin, 1962), p. 147.

5. Robert Friedman, ed., *The Life Millenium: The 100 Most Important Events and People of the Past 1,000 Years* (New York: Life Books, 1998), p. 55.

6. Linda Lear, *Rachel Carson: Witness for Nature* (New York: Henry Holt and Company, 1997), p. 119.

7. Clarence Cottam and Thomas Scott, "A Commentary on *Silent Spring*," *Journal of Wildlife Management*, vol. 27, no. 1, January 1963, p. 151.

8. Carson, *Silent Spring*, pp. 296–297.

## Chapter 2. Childhood in Nature

1. Linda Lear, *Rachel Carson: Witness for Nature* (New York: Henry Holt and Company, 1997), p. 16.

2. Liberty H. Bailey, *The Nature-Study Idea* (New York: Doubleday, Page & Company, 1903), p. 15.

3. Ibid., p. 31.

4. "Bison," *Microsoft Encarta Encyclopedia 2001*. 1993-2000 Microsoft Corporation; "Bison," p. 1.

5. *Pennsylvania Game Commission*, "Extinct Species: Passenger Pigeon," <http://www.pgc.state.pa.us/pgc/cwp/view.asp?a=486&q=152540&pp=12&n=1> (February 20, 2005).

6. Lear, p. 17.

7. Ibid., p. 16.

8. Ibid., p. 19.

## Chapter 3. Becoming a Scientist

1. Linda Lear, *Rachel Carson: Witness for Nature* (New York: Henry Holt and Company, 1997), p. 32.

2. Ibid., p. 25.

3. Ibid., p. 29.

4. Ibid., pp. 33–34.

5. Paul Brooks, *Rachel Carson: The Writer at Work* (San Francisco: Sierra Club Books, 1972), p. 19.

6. Ibid., pp. 20–21.

7. Ibid., p. 53.

8. Ibid., p. 66.

9. Ibid., p. 72.

## Chapter 4. Writing, Science, and Government Work

1. Linda Lear, *Rachel Carson: Witness for Nature* (New York: Henry Holt and Company, 1997), p. 78.

2. Paul Brooks, *Rachel Carson: The Writer at Work* (San Francisco: Sierra Club Books, 1972), p. 22.

3. Ibid.

4. Lear, p. 79.

5. Brooks, p. 23.

6. Lear, p. 83.

7. Ibid., p. 86.

8. Rachel Carson, "Undersea," *The Atlantic Monthly* Magazine, Volume CLX, July-December (Rumford Press, 1937), p. 322.

9. Lear, p. 94.

10. Rachel L. Carson, *Under the Sea Wind* (New York: Truman Talley Books, 1941), pp. 10–14.

## Chapter 5. Writing the Sea

1. Paul Brooks, *Rachel Carson: The Writer at Work* (San Francisco: Sierra Club Books, 1972), pp. 73–75.

2. Ibid., p. 78.

3. Rachel L. Carson, *Guarding Our Wildlife Resources*, "Conservation in Action Series," number 5 (Washington, D.C.: US Government Printing Office, 1948), <http://training.fws.gov/history/Carson/guarding.pdf> (February 24, 2005).

4. Linda Lear, *Rachel Carson: Witness for Nature* (New York: Henry Holt and Company, 1997), p. 135–136.

5. Brooks, pp. 118–119.

6. Rachel Carson, *The Sea Around Us* (New York: Oxford University Press, 1950), p. 126.

7. Brooks, p. 161.

## Chapter 6. The Age of Pesticides

1. G. Fischer, "The Nobel Prize in Physiology or Medicine 1948 Presentation Speech" from *Nobel Lectures, Physiology or Medicine 1942–1962* (Amsterdam: Elsevier Publishing, 1964), <http://nobelprize.org/medicine/laureates/a948/press.html> (June 19, 2004).

2. "Twentieth-Century Insect Control," *Agricultural Research Service of the United States Department of Agriculture*, <http://www.ars.usda.gov/is/timeline/insect.htm?pf=1> (July 15, 2004).

3. Fischer, p. 3.

4. "Useful Fog," *Time*, July 23, 1945, pp. 90–92.

5. Ibid.

6. "War on Insects," *Time*, August 27, 1945, p. 65.

7. Christopher J. Bosso, *Pesticides and Politics: The Life Cycle of a Public Issue* (Pittsburgh: University of Pittsburgh Press, 1987), p. 45.

8. Linda Lear, *Rachel Carson: Witness for Nature* (New York: Henry Holt and Company, 1997), p. 119.

9. "Useful Fog," p. 92.

10. Bosso, p. 46.

11. Paul Brooks, *Rachel Carson: The Writer at Work* (San Francisco: Sierra Club Books, 1972), p. 235.

12. Lear, p. 319.

13. Ibid., p. 368.

## Chapter 7. *Silent Spring*

1. Rachel Carson, *Silent Spring* (Boston: Houghton Mifflin, 1962), p. 1.

2. Ibid., p. 2.

3. Ibid.

4. Ibid., p. 3.

5. Ibid., pp. 22–23.

6. George J. Wallace, "Insecticides and Birds," *Audubon Magazine*, vol. 61, no. 1, January-February 1959, p. 10.

7. Ibid.

8. Carson, *Silent Spring*, p. 108.

9. George J. Wallace, "Another Year of Robin Losses on a University Campus," *Audubon Magazine*, vol. 62, no. 2, March-April 1960, p. 66.

10. Carson, *Silent Spring*, p. 120.

11. "Great Lakes Fact Sheet: The Fall and Rise of Osprey Populations in the Great Lakes Basin," *Government of Canada*, n.d., <http://www.on.ec.gc.ca/wildlife/factsheets/fs_osprey-e.html> (February 23, 2005).

12. Carson, *Silent Spring*, p. 165.

13. Ibid., p. 166.

14. Ibid., p. 272.

15. "Toxicological Profile for DDT, DDE, and DDD," *Agency for Toxic Substances and Disease Registry* (Atlanta: U. S. Department of Health and Human Services, 2002), <http://www.atsdr.cdc.gov/toxprofiles/tp35-c6.pdf> (February 23, 2005).

16. Carson, *Silent Spring*, p. 229.

17. Ibid., p. 296.

## Chapter 8. "Noisy Summer"

1. John M. Lee, "'Silent Spring' Is Now Noisy Summer," *The New York Times*, July 22, 1962, Business and Finance, p. 1.

2. Ibid., p. 11.

3. Linda Lear, *Rachel Carson: Witness for Nature* (New York: Henry Holt and Company, 1997), p. 417.

4. Ibid., p. 419.

5. Ibid., p. 431.

6. Rachel Carson, *Silent Spring* (Boston: Houghton Mifflin, 1962), p. 12.

7. Paul Brooks, *Rachel Carson: The Writer at Work* (San Francisco: Sierra Club Books, 1972), p. 305.

8. Lear, p. 449.

9. "Schweitzer Medalists," *Animal Welfare Institute,* <www.awionline.org/Schweitzer> (February 21, 2005).

10. Brooks, pp. 310–311.

11. Lear, p. 454.

12. Ibid., p. 464.

## Chapter 9. "A Tide of Environmental Consciousness"

1. "DDT Ban Takes Effect," EPA press release, December 31, 1972, <http://www.epa.gov/history/topics/ddt/01.htm> (July 10, 2004).

2. Linda Lear, *Rachel Carson: Witness for Nature* (New York: Henry Holt and Company, 1997), p. 477.

3. *Federal Insecticide, Fungicide, and Rodenticide Act, 7 U.S.C s/s 136 et seq* (U.S. Environmental Protection Agency, 1996), <http://www.epa.gov/region5/defs/html/fifra.htm> (August 3, 2004).

4. "Introduction by Vice President Al Gore," <http://clinton2.nara.gov/WH/EOP/OVP/24hours/Carson.html> (February 16, 2005).

5. "Medal of Freedom: Presidential Medal of Freedom Recipient Rachel Louise Carson," <http://www.medaloffreedom.com/RachelCarson.htm> (February 21, 2005).

6. "The Bald Eagle Is Back!" U.S. Fish and Wildlife Service News Release, <http://www.fws.gov/r9extaff/eaglejuly2.html> (February 21, 2005).

7. Donald L. Beaver, "Recovery of an American Robin Population After Earlier DDT Use," <http://elibrary.unm.edu/sora/JFO/v051n03/p0220-p0228.html> (January 27, 2005).

# Glossary

**aldrin**—A chlorinated hydrocarbon used as an insecticide.

**algae**—Simple stemless water plants.

**bioaccumulation**—The tendency for a compound to accumulate in an organism's tissues.

**buoy**—An anchored float serving as a navigation marker.

**camaraderie**—Trust and sociability among friends.

**carcinogen**—A substance that causes cancer.

**chlorinated hydrocarbons**—Long-lasting, man-made, chemical compounds. Many were used as pesticides.

**conservation**—The care protection and management of natural resources.

**cumulative**—Increasing in amount, accumulated.

**diatoms**—Microscopic algae that is a food for much marine life.

**dichloro-diphenyl-dichloroethylene**—DDE, a by-product of DDT in soil, water, or living tissue.

**dichloro-diphenyl-trichloroethane**—DDT, the first chlorinated hydrocarbon used as a pesticide.

**dieldrin**—A chlorinated hydrocarbon used as an insecticide.

**ecology**—The branch of biology that deals with the relationship between living things and their environment.

**embryo**—An unborn or unhatched offspring.

**epidemic**—A rapidly spreading disease.

**eradicate**—To destroy or get rid of completely.

**food chain**—The path of food consumption of transferring energy from one organism to another.

**Great Depression**—A period of economic collapse in the United States beginning in 1929 and continuing to about 1940.

**larva**—A stage of development of an insect. The plural is larvae.

**leukemia**—A disease affecting blood-forming organs.

**lichen**—A plant made up of a fungus and an alga.

**malaria**—An infectious disease carried by female mosquitoes.

**migration**—The movement of a population from one place to another.

**naturalist**—A person who studies nature.

**nauseated**—Feeling sick to your stomach.

**oceanographic**—Of the study of the oceans.

**organism**—An individual living plant or animal.

**ornithologist**—A scientist who studies birds.

**osprey**—A fish eagle.

**pesticide**—A chemical intended to kill pests such as insects.

**prawn**—A seafood, also know as a large shrimp.

**raptor**—An eagle, osprey, falcon, or other bird of prey. Raptors feed mostly on fish, birds, or other animals.

**sea anemone**—A flower-like sea creature.

**shoal**—A shallow place in the sea.

**species**—A category of living organisms.

**tsunami**—A sea wave caused by an underwater earthquake, landslide, or volcano.

**tumor**—A lump or mass of abnormal tissue.

**typhus**—An infectious disease spread by fleas or lice.

**zoology**—The branch of biology that deals with the scientific study of animals.

# Further Reading

Ehrlich, Amy. *Rachel: The Story of Rachel Carson*. New York: Silver Whistle, 2003.

Glimm, Adele. *Rachel Carson: Protecting Our Earth*. New York: McGraw-Hill, 2000.

Kudlinski, Kathleen. *Rachel Carson: Pioneer of Ecology*. New York: Puffin Books, 1997.

Locker, Thomas. *Rachel Carson: Preserving a Sense of Wonder*. New York: Fulcrum Pub., 2004.

Quaratiello, A. *Rachel Carson: A Biography*. Westport, Conn.: Greenwood, 2004.

Tremblay, E.A. *Rachel Carson: Author/Ecologist*. Broomall, Pa.: Chelsea House, 2003.

Wadsworth, Ginger. *Rachel Carson: Voice for the Earth*. Minneapolis: Lerner, 1992.

# Internet Addresses

**Rachel Carson.org**
http://www.rachelcarson.org/

**The Rachel Carson Homestead**
http://www.rachelcarsonhomestead.org/

**Ecology Hall of Fame: Rachel Carson**
http://www.ecotopia.org/ehof/carson/

**National Wildlife Refuge**
http://www.fws.gov

# Index